TAYLOR SWIFT

BY JILL SHERMAN

AMICUS LEARNING

Inspire is published by
Amicus Learning, an imprint of Amicus
P.O. Box 227
Mankato, MN 56002
www.amicuspublishing.us

Editor: Ana Brauer
Series Designer: Kathleen Petelinsek
Book Designer and Photo Researcher: Emily Dietz

Library of Congress Cataloging-in-Publication Data
Names: Sherman, Jill, author.
Title: Taylor Swift / by Jill Sherman.
Description: Mankato, MN : Amicus Learning, 2025. | Series: Inspire | Includes bibliographical references
    and index. | Audience: Ages 5–9 | Audience: Grades 2–3 | Summary: "Learn about global superstar
    Taylor Swift and her accomplishments in the music industry in this biography packed with photographs
    and fact-filled text suitable for young readers. Includes table of contents, glossary, further resources,
    and index"—Provided by publisher.
Identifiers: LCCN 2024012085 (print) | LCCN 2024012086 (ebook) | ISBN 9798892001076 (library
    binding) | ISBN 9798892001656 (paperback) | ISBN 9798892002233 (ebook)
Subjects: LCSH: Swift, Taylor, 1989—Juvenile literature. | Singers—United States—
    Biography—Juvenile literature. | Country musicians—United States—Biography—
    Juvenile literature.
Classification: LCC ML3930.S989 S57 2025 (print) | LCC ML3930.S989 (ebook) | DDC
    782.42164092 [B]—dc23/eng/20240315
LC record available at https://lccn.loc.gov/2024012085
LC ebook record available at https://lccn.loc.gov/2024012086

Table of Contents

Star Power

Taylor Swift struts across the stage. She's dressed in head-to-toe sparkles. She sings her hit songs. The crowd sings along. They know all the **lyrics** by heart. Swift is one of the biggest pop music stars in the world.

Taylor Swift's fans
are called Swifties.

Swift's song "Christmas Tree Farm"
is based on where she grew up in
Wyomissing, Pennsylvania.

6

Dear Diary

Swift grew up on a Christmas tree farm in Pennsylvania. At school, Swift had few friends. It could be lonely. She wrote poems in her diary. Later, Swift learned to play guitar. Her poems soon became songs.

Breaking In

Swift loved music. Country music was her favorite. She wanted it to be her job. In 2004, Swift moved to and started performing in Nashville, Tennessee. Soon, a **record label** took notice. Swift was going to make her own album.

Swift was just 16 years
old when she released
her first album.

9

In 2007, Swift won Breakthrough Video of the Year for her song "Tim McGraw."

Topping the Charts

Swift's first **single** was titled "Tim McGraw." It hit radio stations in 2006. It was an instant hit. It made it to the music **charts**. This was just the start. Many of Swift's songs became chart-topping hits.

THE LUCKY ONE

In 2009, Swift went on tour with country singer Keith Urban. Later that year, she began her first solo tour for her album *Fearless*.

Pop Star

Swift's first albums were country. But there are many styles, or **genres**, of music. By 2014, Swift wanted to try something new. Her album *1989* was a pop hit. How about rock? Or R&B? Or folk? Swift explored all of these music types on future albums.

Swift performs on stage during her *1989* world tour.

A guitar signed by Swift
was sold to raise money
for a charity that helps
musicians in need.
Epiphone
MUSICARES
Charity Relief Auction
FEBRUARY 5, 2023
11:00AM PT
Julien's
AUCTIONS
taylor swift
lien's
AUCTIONS
juliensauctions.com

Influencer

When Swift speaks, people listen. On social media, she asked her fans to register to vote. That day, 35,000 new voters were registered. Swift also helps **charities** and gives back to the community. In 2023, Swift donated $1 million to Tennessee after it was hit by tornadoes.

IN THE PUBLIC EYE

Fans want to know all about Swift. When she dates someone, it is big news. Swift writes songs about her life. Fans look to her music to know her better.

Superstar

It's not just fans who love Swift's songs. *Billboard* ranks the most popular songs every week. In October 2022, she became the first musician to claim all top ten spots on their list. She also has 14 Grammy Awards. She's even won Album of the Year four times!

Taylor's Version

Swift announces *Speak Now (Taylor's Version)* during the Eras tour in 2023.

who owns a song? Every song has a **master** recording. Swift's record label owned her masters. They could sell her music. But Swift wanted to own her music. She re-recorded her old albums. She even added new songs. She released the albums as "Taylor's Version."

On tour, Swift changed her
clothes to match each of
her albums. This sparkly
outfit is for *Midnights*.

Eras

Seeing Swift perform live is a blast! In 2023, she began her Eras Tour. It celebrates her musical career. Fans came dressed like Swift. They traded friendship bracelets of their favorite songs. The concerts were her best yet!

ON THE BIG SCREEN
Fans who missed the tour could watch *Taylor Swift: The Eras Tour* in movie theaters. The movie made $267.1 million!

TAYLOR SWIFT

Birthday: December 13, 1989

Hometown: Wyomissing, Pennsylvania

AWARDS THROUGH 2024

Grammys: 14

Billboard Music Awards: 49

MTV Video Music Awards: 30

Emmy Awards: 1

ACCOMPLISHMENTS

Wrote and Directed *All Too Well: A Short Film* (2021)

Only person to win Album of the Year four times

Spotify's most played artist (2023)

charities Groups that help people in need.

chart A ranking of the most popular music.

genre A particular type or style of music.

lyrics The words to a song.

master The official, original recording of a song.

record label A business that records and promotes music.

single A song that is released separately from an album.

GLOSSARY

READ MORE

Olsen, Elsie. **Taylor Swift.** Minneapolis: Checkerboard Library, 2021.

Vegara, Maria Isabel Sanchez. **Taylor Swift.** London: Frances Lincoln Children's Books. 2024.

ON THE WEB

All Music
https://www.allmusic.com/artist/mn0000472102

Official Website of Taylor Swift
https://www.taylorswift.com/

INDEX

About the Author

Jill Sherman writes books about pop stars, baby animals, and robots. She loves that writing allows her to research and learn about new topics. In addition to writing books, Jill sews her own clothes, creates crossword puzzles, and codes in JavaScript.

She listened to all of Taylor Swift's music while writing this book.